SiLENT PiCTURES

a skewed look at showbiz

Katie Maratta

LONE EAGLE

Scene 1
Take 2
they're small

SILENT PICTURES

Lone Eagle Publishing Company
2337 Roscomare Road — Suite Nine
Los Angeles, CA 90077-1815
310/471-8066 • FAX 310/471-4969

Printed in the United States of America

Cover design by Heidi Frieder
Cover drawing by Katie Maratta

Library in Congress Cataloging in Publication Data

Maratta, Kate.
    SILENT PICTURES / by Katie Maratta
        p.   cm.
    ISBN 0-943728-49-5 : $9.95
      1. Motion Picture Industry — Caricatures and cartoons.
    2. Television — Caricatures and cartoons. I. Title.
    NC1429.M4219A4   1992
    741.5'973—dc20

                                  92-35013
                                    CIP

Special thanks to Amy Goldman Koss,
the folks at Emmy Magazine, Irv Letofsky, Mark Anderson,
and, especially, Peter Maratta

THE DINNER PARTY

THE PITCH

THE POST-PITCH DEPRESSION

THE 2 KINDS of HOLLYWOOD PROJECTS

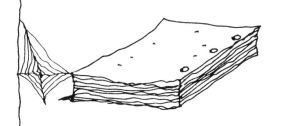

the kind that
don't go anywhere

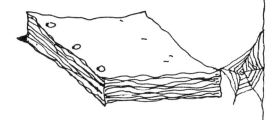

the kind that
go nowhere

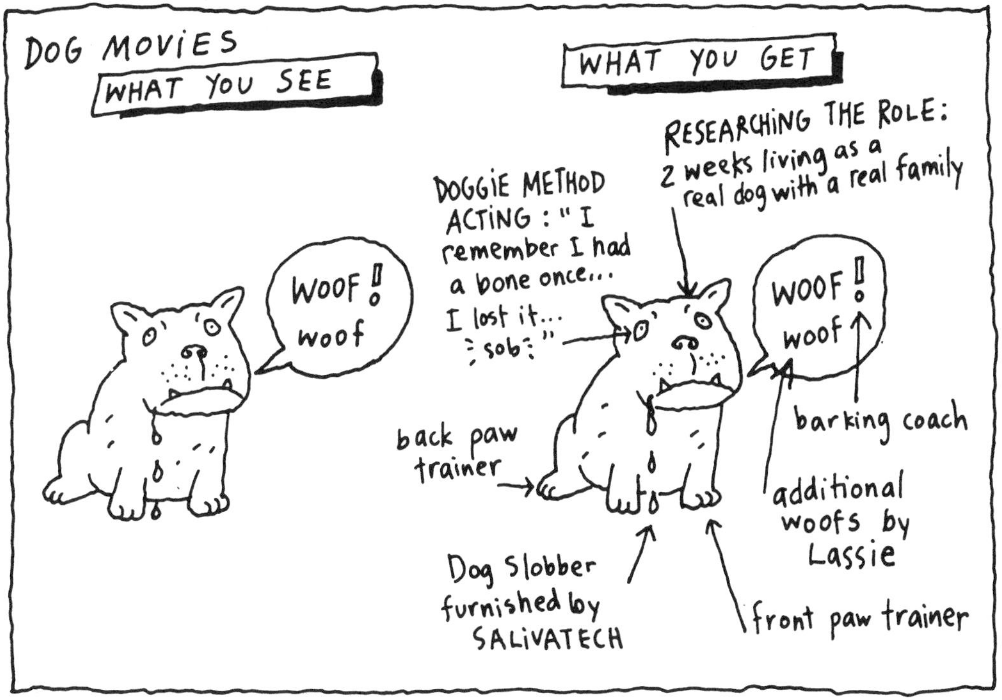
DOG MOVIES
WHAT YOU SEE
WOOF! woof
WHAT YOU GET
RESEARCHING THE ROLE: 2 weeks living as a real dog with a real family
DOGGIE METHOD ACTING: "I remember I had a bone once... I lost it... sob"
WOOF! woof
back paw trainer
barking coach
additional woofs by Lassie
Dog Slobber furnished by SALIVATECH
front paw trainer

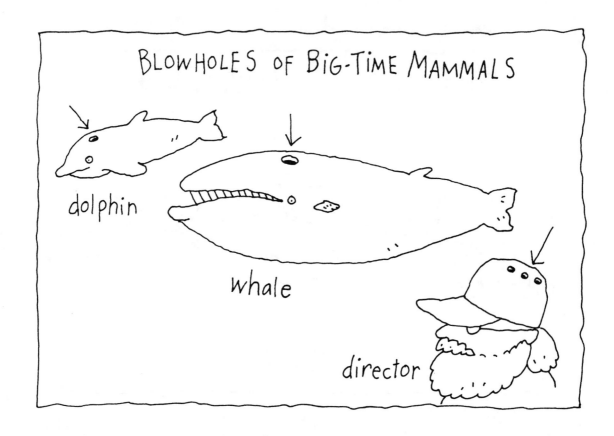

"HE JUST WANTS TO MEET YOU"

: or :

why network programming executives
have such big desks

1.

2.

FE FI FO FUM

3.

NEW IN TOWN

THE AGENT

MARATTA

ASPIRING ACTOR

A COPPOLA DIRECTORS

commercial director

TEXTURE.

INTENSITY.

HUMOR.

THAT'S WHAT HAS
TYPIFIED MY WORK.

ESPECIALLY THE
TALKING PANTY
SHIELDS SPOT.

EDITOR

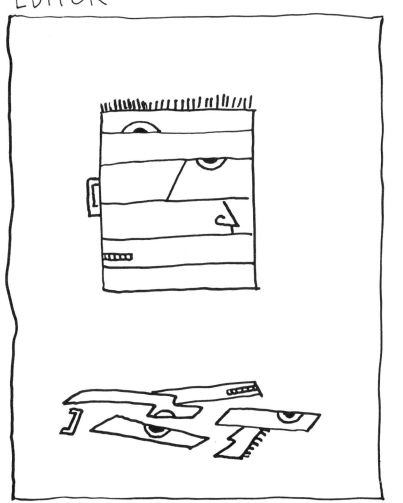

LOCATION MANAGERS

MARATTA

ANOTHER SUCCESSFUL SCREENWRITER

4 YEARS, 120 PAGES, 8 REWRITES.
ITS A MASTERPIECE — IT'S
ABOUT A BOY
AND A PACK
OF WILD
DOGS

I HATE DOGS —

DID I SAY DOGS?
I MEANT DOLPHINS.

SITCOM ACTOR FACTORY (SOMEWHERE IN THE VALLEY)

MARATTA

ACTOR'S WIFE

it's hard being married to
   a quote unquote star —

sure, it's glamorous
   and exciting —

but if you're not careful,
  you can lose track of
   what's really important —

that's why I opened
 my boutique on
  Melrose —

after all, I'm a person, too...
 with talent and feelings —
you know, all that stuff —

KRISHNAWOODI

A DEITY WORSHIPPED BY SOME HILL TRIBES.

THE EMBLEMS IN HIS HANDS SYMBOLIZE THE
FOUR DISCIPLINES: WRITING, PRODUCING, DIRECTING,
AND STARRING.

THE DEITY IS MOST OFTEN REPRESENTED AS
DANCING ALL THE WAY TO THE BANK WITH ONE
FOOT UPRAISED AND THE OTHER CRUSHING
THE PROSTRATE DEMON OF SELF-RESTRAINT.

MARATTA

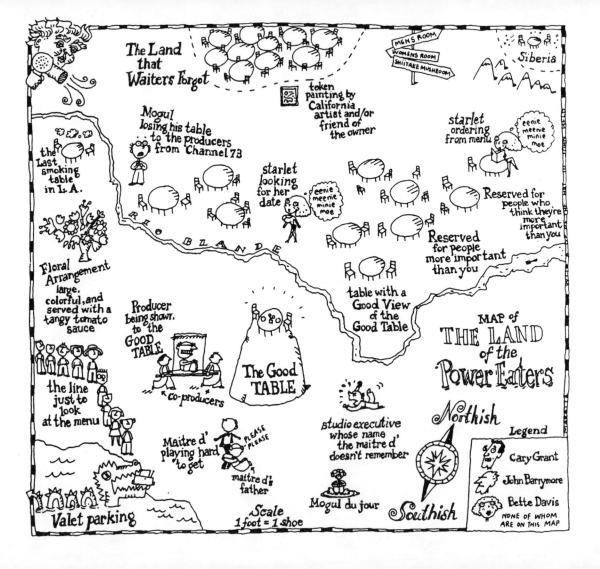

A FAMILIAR SCENE

EVERYTHING LOOKS **SO** GOOD! WHAT A PLACE! WHAT DO **YOU** RECOMMEND? HUH? MR. WEEVIL?

BRAND NEW PERSON

TRENDY DISHES

OH, THE LOBSTER A LA CRISCO IS **EXCELLENT**! AND YOU **MUST** TRY THE SHRIMP WITH OREO COOKIES AND THE TURNIPS IN TRIPE SAUCE!

ASSUMES PROPER WORSHIPFUL ATTITUDE

WELL, OK. SINCE YOU SAY SO. I'LL HAVE THE SHRIMP AND THE TURNIPS AND THE LOBSTER. I GUESS.

VERY GOOD. AND FOR YOU, MR. WEEVIL?

JUST SOME BROTH. AND A CRACKER. MAKE THAT ½ A CRACKER. HEH HEH

HE FORGOT LUNCH LESSON #3 **ALWAYS** MAKE THE **MOST** IMPORTANT PERSON ORDER **FIRST**. DON'T LET THIS HAPPEN TO YOU. WATCH FOR LESSONS IN LUNCH.

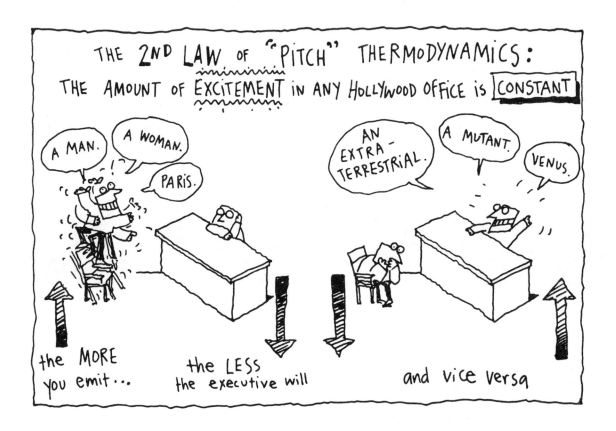

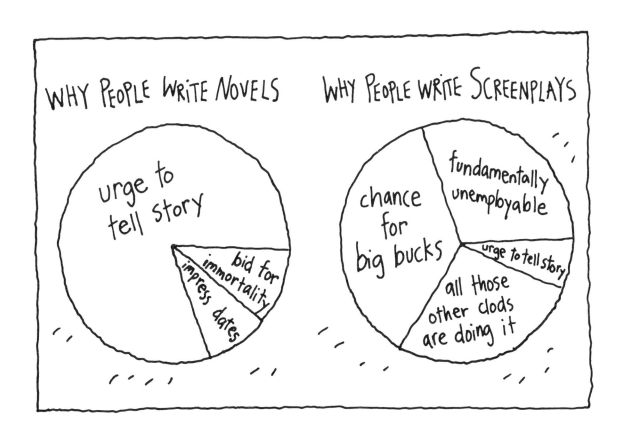

SIZE OF
the SCRIPT

YOUR LINES
in the
SCRIPT

SIZE OF
YOUR CONTRACT

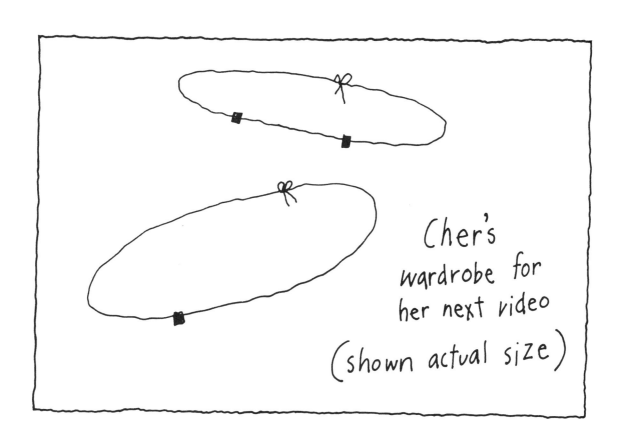

Cher's
wardrobe for
her next video

(shown actual size)

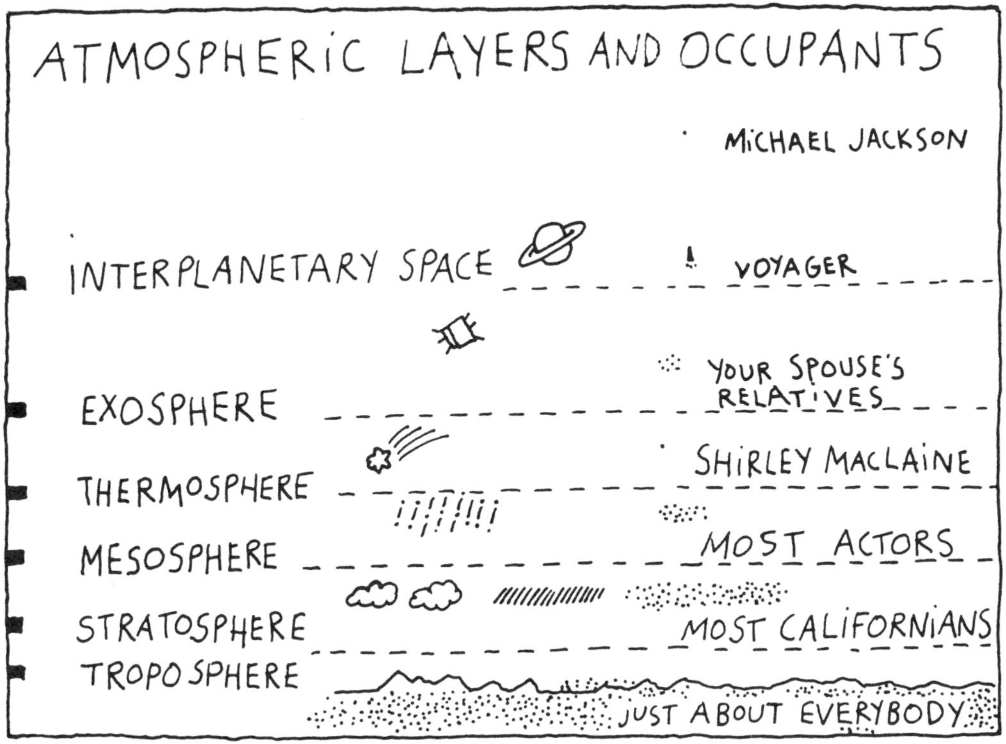
ATMOSPHERIC LAYERS AND OCCUPANTS
MICHAEL JACKSON
INTERPLANETARY SPACE
VOYAGER
YOUR SPOUSE'S RELATIVES
EXOSPHERE
SHIRLEY MACLAINE
THERMOSPHERE
MOST ACTORS
MESOSPHERE
MOST CALIFORNIANS
STRATOSPHERE
TROPOSPHERE
JUST ABOUT EVERYBODY

Star

Star promoting
his latest movie

Star promoting
his latest movie
that he has a piece of

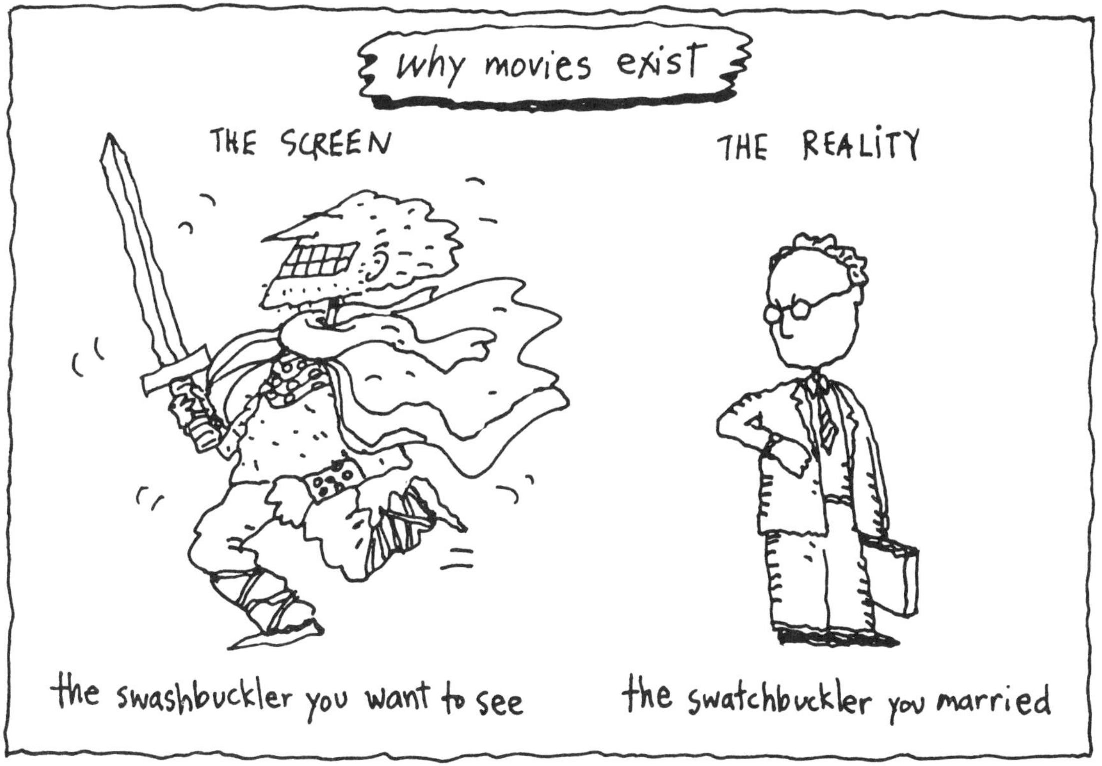
why movies exist
THE SCREEN
THE REALITY
the swashbuckler you want to see
the swatchbuckler you married

THE OUT-OF-TOWNER

IT'S TOO HOT, TOO SMOGGY,
THERE'S TOO MUCH TRAFFIC,
TOO MANY CRAZIES, AND
EVERYTHING'S TOO
EXPENSIVE.

BUT MY FEET ARE SMALLER
THAN BETTE DAVIS'.

OUT-OF-TOWNER   (from New York)

Network Executives' Exercise Class

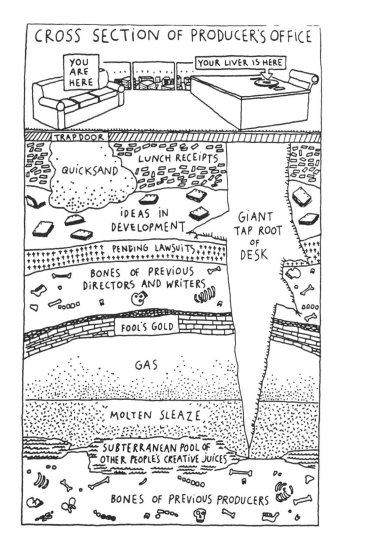

A WARNING FOR NETWORK EXECUTIVES

if you get poor reception

if you have no vertical hold

if you're too bright

MARATTA

it can lead to

PREHISTORIC HOLLYWOOD

THE PRIMORDIAL SCHMOOZE

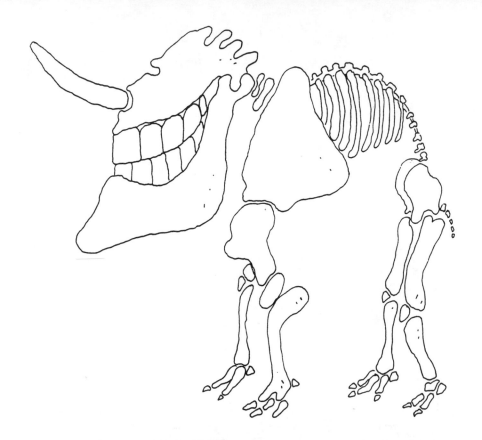

GREAT HORNED WALK-ON

A minor, bicoastal lizard. Although fearsome in profile,
its huge tusks and teeth were adapted only for eating
Belgian endive, shiitake mushrooms, and sun-dried tomatoes.

WOOLLY BLOCKBUSTER

CIGAROSAUR

BRAIN #2

BRAIN #1

TWO CIGAROSAURS MEETING

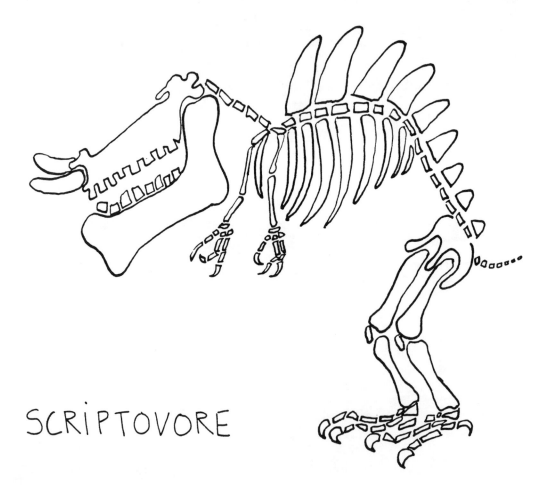

SCRIPTOVORE

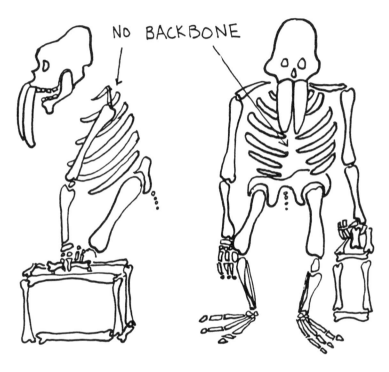

SABER-TOOTHED ACCOUNTANT

This sly, quick-footed dinosaur thrived in the area, stalking its prey at dusk at watering holes & feeding grounds. By means of an insidious hunting technique called "representation", the Sleazodon is believed to have gradually & systematically drained its quarry's vital fluids, "dropping" the doomed creature when it was no longer "hot". Large concentrations of Sleazodon skulls have been found in the vicinity of the Beverly Hills Polo Lounge.

SLEAZODON

MARATTA

RECEIPT –

SPIRIT OF CHRISTMAS PAST

PETTY CASH -
Spirit of Christmas Present

REJOICE! FOR ON THIS
DAY BY FUDGING YOUR
MILEAGE YOU CAN PICK
UP YOUR BOYFRIEND &
BLOW THE EXTRA DOUGH
AT "THE IVY"

POINTS.

Spirit of Christmas Future

HARK! The negative costs are off-set! Glory to the one half of one percent therever after. Blessed is the back-end cable deal for it shall pay off the Porsche 911 SC.

Little known departments in the STUDIO BUREAUCRACY
OFFICE OF UNACCOUNTABLY VAPID ROLES FOR WOMEN
GRATUITOUS & GOOEY VIOLENCE SECTION
A BRANCH OF THE NEEDLESS OBSCENITIES BUREAU
TITLES DEPARTMENT
BAD DIVISION
how about "DYING YOUNG?"

NETWORK MOVING SERIES TO NEW TIME SLOT

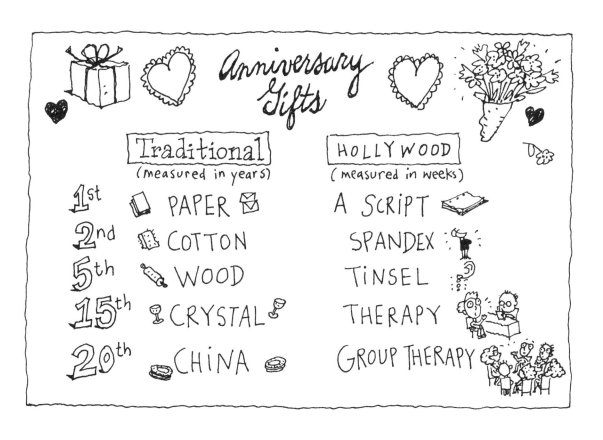

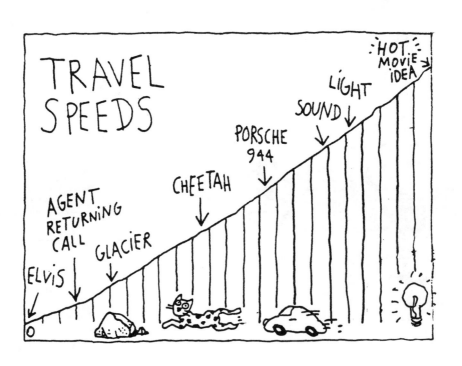

KNOT TYING FOR THE RICH & FAMOUS

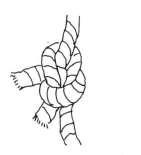

THE SHEET BEND

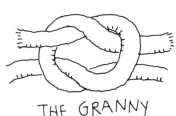

THE GRANNY KNOT

THE PRENUPTIAL AGREEMENT

ACTIVITY PAGE FOR CHILDREN OF THE RICH AND FAMOUS

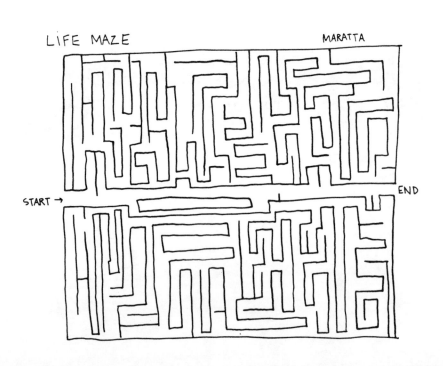

LIFE MAZE · MARATTA

START → · END

STREET SIGNS

DOUBLE CROSSING

NO CREATIVE OUTLET

YIELD

RIGHT TURN ON RED
IF YOU FEEL LIKE IT

HOLLYWOOD CALORIE CHART

ACTIVITY	CALORIES BURNED
COUNTING THE FLASHES ON YOUR ANSWERING MACHINE	... 140
EXITING AT STUDIO CITY WHERE 134 MEETS 101	... 6,200
COLLABORATING	... 12,000
STANDING IN A DOORWAY DURING A 5.2	... 100,000
TRYING TO DECIDE WHETHER IT'S WORTH RUNNING TO THE DOORWAY	... 102,000
WATCHING THE INTERVIEW ON "ENTERTAINMENT TONIGHT" WITH A	... 236,000
GUY WHO SOLD THE VERY FIRST SCREENPLAY HE EVER WROTE	... 96,752,000

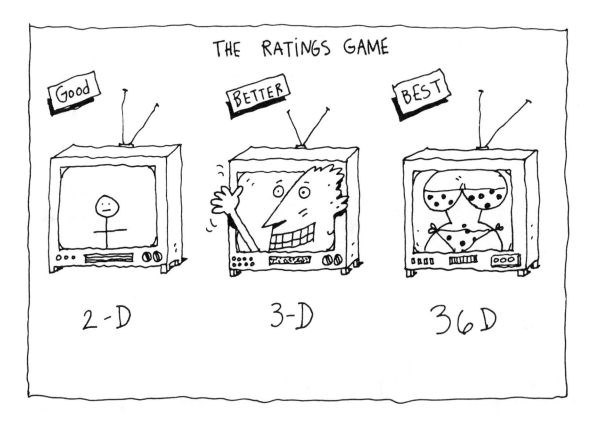

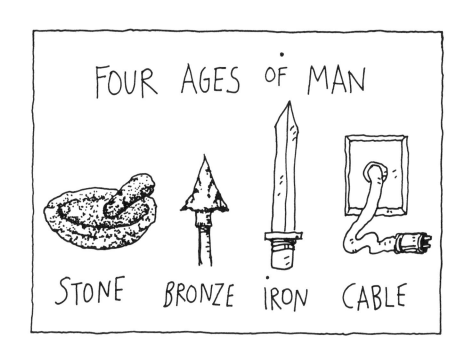

Edgar Allan Poe – the first guy to package his clients
LOOK. YOU WANT THE PIT, AND YOU'LL GET THE PIT, BUT YOU HAVE TO TAKE THE PENDULUM, TOO!
oh, ok.

Celebrity Books We'd like to See

FRANK ZAPPA'S Book of Baby Names

1,001 Names for *Your* Bundle o' Joy Like "Thorazine" or "Yikes!"

ACTORS GIVE THANKS
At least I'm not doing tv.
At least I'm not doing commercials.
At least I'm not doing crime re-enactment shows.
At least I'm not watching crime re-enactment shows.
MOVIE STAR
SIT COM STAR
COMMERCIAL STAR
CRIME RE-ENACTMENT STAR

How the IRS sorts Michael Eisner's lunch receipts
D.Ducktible
non-D.Ducktible

HOW YOU KNOW YOU'RE BORED...

video title scan syndrome

YOU GO TO THE VIDEO STORE

HOW YOU KNOW YOU'RE REALLY BORED

TAP TAP

YOU HANG AROUND THE "JUST-RETURNED" RACK

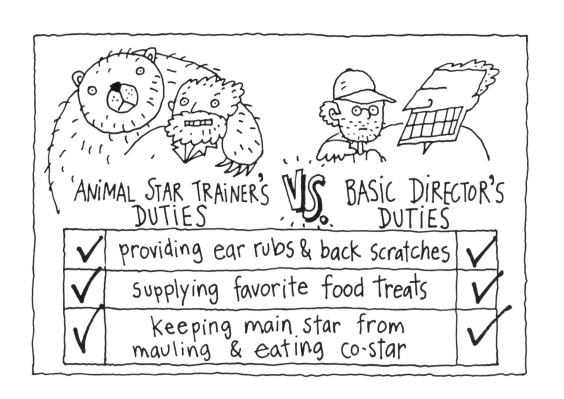

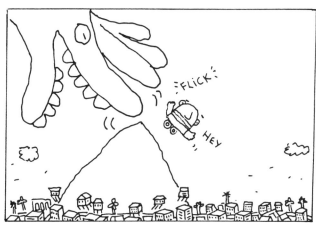

GATHERING PEOPLE FOR A PROJECT

To Get a Writer

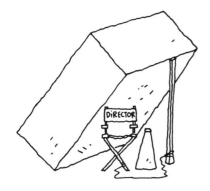

Promise him a director job...next time.

To Get a Director

Bait the trap with the screenplay you just got.

To Get a Star

Tie the director to a stake and his cries will draw the big talent to the pit.

MARATTA

THE MIRRORED DESK TOP

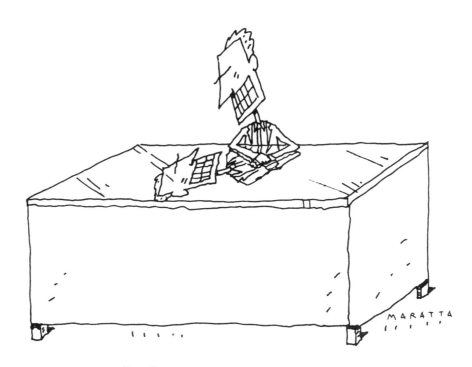

For talk show hosts who can't
get enough of their favorite guest

COLORIZATION COMPUTER & TECHNICIAN

Kevin Costner's most challenging role

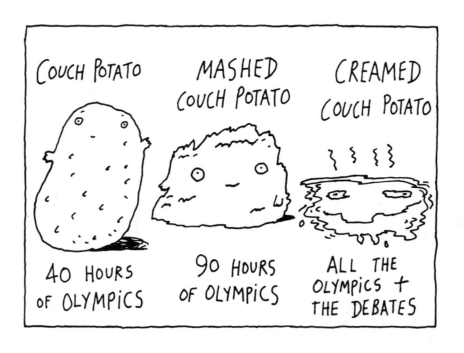

HOLLYWOOD EXECUTIVE SPORT
At dawn, I go out and ride the backs of my staff until I'm exhausted. I call it "serfing".

MEET & GREET at the EMMYS

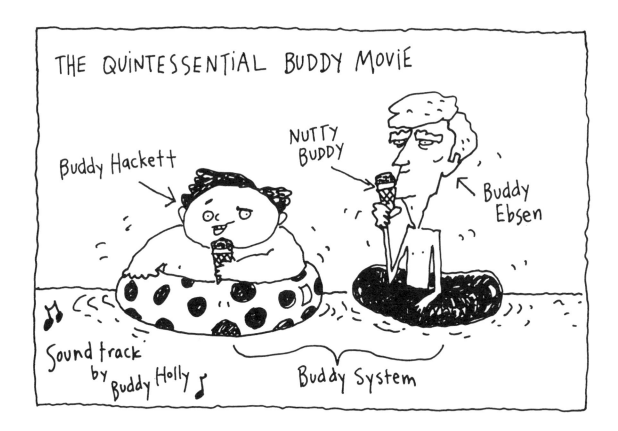

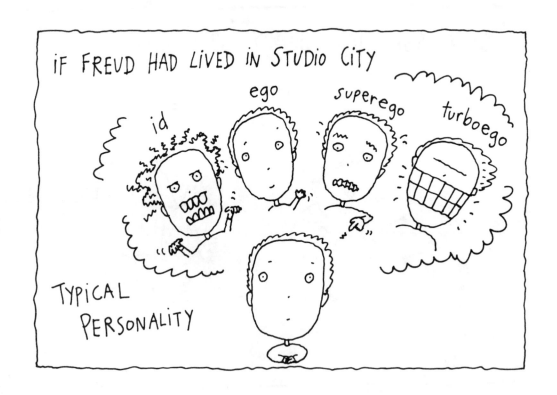

THE HOLLYWOOD OFFICE WE SEE
big phone
posters of big hits he was involved with
big desk
THE HOLLYWOOD OFFICE WE'D LIKE TO SEE
big phone
posters of big hits he said "NO" to
big desk

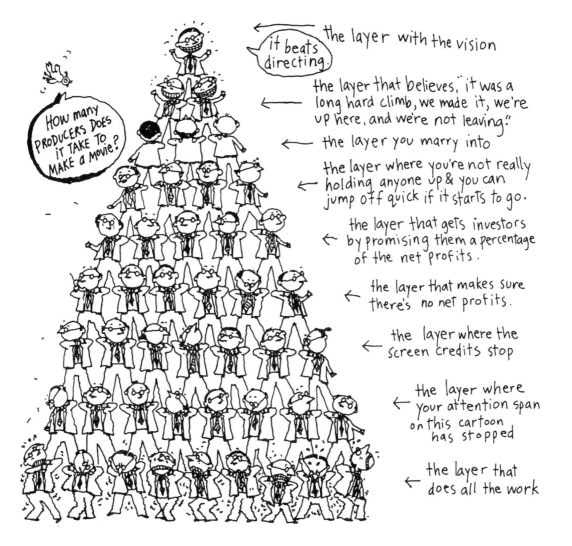

LIFE OF A SCREENPLAY

WHAT YOU WRITE

WHAT YOU REWRITE

WHAT YOUR AGENT READS

WHAT THE STUDIO BUYS

GUY who's
SOLD OUT

GROUP
ACCUSING
HIM OF SELLING OUT

GROUP HOPING
TO SELL OUT

How Creative control works

BACK TO FILM SCHOOL

Your chair   Your film noir crayon set   Your Lunch money

BLACK · BLACKISH · MOSTLY BLACK · OFF-BLACK · BURNT BLACK · TOO BLACK · BLACK WITH A HINT OF BLACK

STRUGGLING
SCREENWRITER

SCREENWRITER
WITH AGENT

SCREENWRITER
WITH SCREEN CREDIT

AND WEEVIL WENT INTO THE WILDERNESS AND ENDURETH MANY HARDSHIPS IN SEARCH OF THE PROMISED INVESTOR.

WHAT IS THIS?!

SUPER SAVER.

© 1987 MARATTA   10-27

WHAT IS THAT?!

WEATHER.

WELCOME TO JEFFVILLE OHIO

NOW, LET ME GET THIS STRAIGHT. I BUY YOUR STOCK AND, IN EXCHANGE, I DON'T GET TO HELP MAKE THE MOVIE, I DON'T MAKE ANY MONEY OFF THE MOVIE, AND I DON'T EVEN GET IN FOR FREE?

DON'T YOU LOVE IT? SIGN HERE

JEFF

THE AUDITION

ACADEMY AWARDS NIGHT AIR QUALITY
SERIOUSLY
LUNCH
REALLY
BEAUTIFUL
LOVE YA
CALL ME
CALL ME
GREAT
GREAT
LUNCH
LUNCH
LUNCH
THE BEST
TERRIFIC
GREAT
CALL ME
3RD STAGE SCHMOOZE ALERT
unhealthful for sensitive persons

5 WAYS TO SELL A SCREENPLAY

1. Commit a crime.

2. It's easier to sell a book, so write a book. (about what? See No. 1.)

3. Collaborate with someone who's already sold a screenplay. (Careful. This could lead you to No. 1.)

4. Name the hero in your script after the executive you want to buy it.

5. Be a famous star with your own production company.

MARATTA

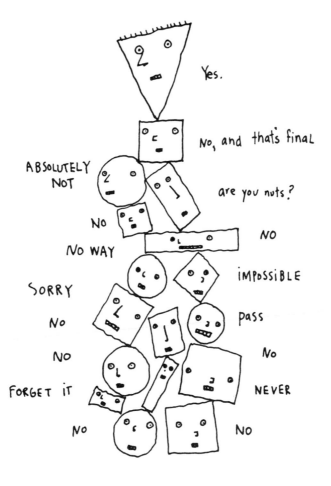

Yes.

No, and that's final

ABSOLUTELY NOT

are you nuts?

NO

NO

NO WAY

IMPOSSIBLE

SORRY

pass

NO

NO

NO

NEVER

FORGET IT

NO

NO

HOW A MOVIE GETS MADE

KUBLAI KHAN and OLLIE

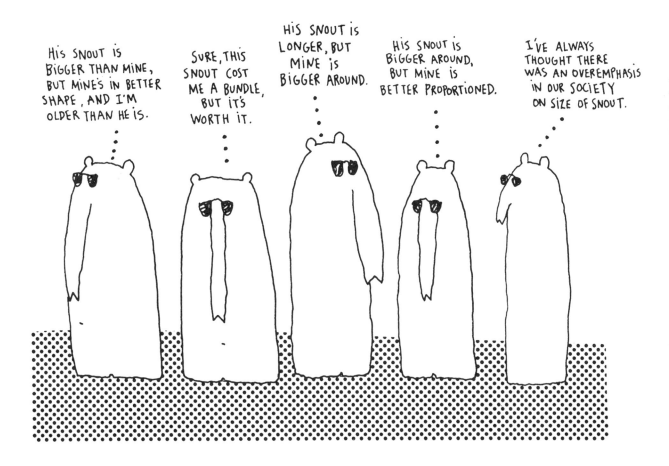

WARNING: THIS CARTOON CONTAINS ADULT LANGUAGE AND ADULT SITUATIONS.
WITH THE MONEY WE SAVED ON THE WASHER-DRYER I CAN GET A "MULCH-MASTER".
OUR ESTIMATED TAX PAYMENT IS DUE AND THE 12 MONTH DEFERRED 1% SALES TAX ON OUR MUTUAL FUND KICKS IN THIS WEEK.
NC-17
no children
hey, even grown-ups can't take this stuff.

BEST: WIDE RELEASE
Seattle
San Francisco
Denver
Detroit
Chicago
New York
Philadelphia
Washington
Phoenix
Atlanta
L.A.
Dallas
San Diego
Miami
GOOD: LIMITED RELEASE
L.A.
New York
BAD: REALLY LIMITED RELEASE
Bluefield, West Virginia
WORST: REALLY LIMITED RELEASE...
Bluefield, West Virginia
...ON THE FIRST DAY OF HUNTING SEASON

MEMORIAL DAY WEEKEND MOVIEGOER PROFILE
YOUNG, TRENDSETTING, AND THEY DIDN'T GET THEIR DEPOSIT IN ON TIME ON THE BEACH HOUSE

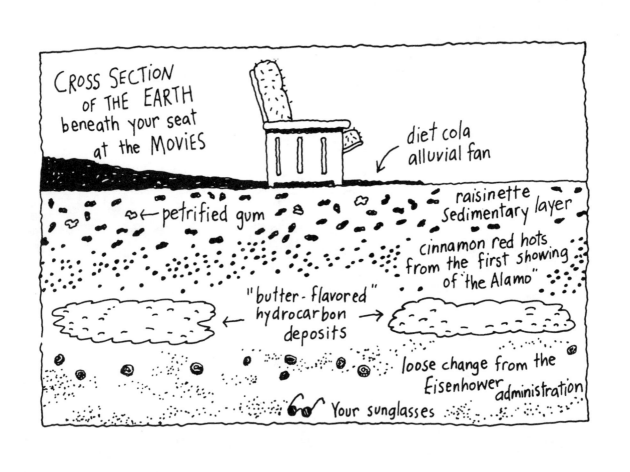